Table of Contents

The Six Hats of the Worship Leader

Preface

Many church leadership books today seem to focus heavily on the language of the corporate world. Throw a creative worship leader into the mix and vertigo sets in for all involved. Why? Creative leaders simply think differently. If you want to learn how to better explain your worship leadership to those in charge, this book is for you. If your role is leading worship leaders, the language shared in this book aims to help you take your team to their next level.

My name is Rich Kirkpatrick. I'm a family man; I'm married to my best friend and we have two kids who are nearly grown. I am a writer and blogger. I also play keys and sing on my church's worship team, so I know how to be the second-fiddle guy when I am not speaking, leading worship, or doing other upfront ministry leadership.

I have served in full-time ministry for nearly two decades as a worship leader and pastor. My passion is and has been the local church—*supporting pastors, worship leaders, tech directors, and creative leaders.* I get to talk to people like you nearly every day and am honored to be both a *challenger* and *encourager.*

And it all started because of pizza.

I was a twenty-year-old pizza delivery guy with a love for music, and I volunteered in my church's choir. After I reworked and hand-copied a shoddy custom choral arrangement, my worship pastor took notice and offered me a job. I went from delivering pizzas to working on his staff.

As the years have passed, I have been part of church plants, mega-churches, multi-site services, and have led hundreds volunteers. I have made many mistakes along the way, and have found that I could not do it all on my own—whether as a leader of a mega-church department with multiple staff, or as a church-planting worship leader with fifty people.

In this book you will find wisdom that many have already implemented, but perhaps never articulated quite in this way. *The entertaining difference here is that I understand you, the creative leader.* You are left to organize your world without a language to describe what you do, let alone to help trouble-shoot it. And if you are a lead pastor or leader in your local church, my hope is that this will provoke conversations about what it really takes to put on a weekend service and make it great.

With church planters and the growth of multi-site church campuses, this language is all the more needed. How does one duplicate and reproduce effective creative ministry? Whether you are trying to help your youth group grow, or you're hoping to expand to another site, the problems to solve are similar, even if the scale or scope is not.

Here in the preface, I will lay out a summary of the Six Hats, so you can begin right away to speak the language. I have found that there are six roles or hats that take place in leading the fifty-two weekend services in worship. Learning what these roles are and casting them well is the key to growing a team, and preventing burnout and mounting frustration.

Leading worship is more than just a plat-form-driven event. There are people to recruit, schedules to keep, projects to manage, and communication to focus. On top of all the "tasks," there is the primary need for spiritual direction of all the people who make up a worship team. Learning how to leverage which of the six roles you should keep for yourself, and which you should delegate, can be the difference maker in sustaining and growing a team that can weather change.

In a smaller setting, people will surely wear more than one hat and most likely will all be volunteers. As a ministry grows, some paid staff will likely be employed to wear the hats that require more time or specialization.

The Six Hats

- *Worship Leader:* This individual's role is to be the upfront face, as well as an intuitively gifted individual who can engage a congregation.

- *Music Director:* The details of music are important and led with the direction of rehearsal, preparation of charts, and supervision of the direction of the "sound" of the worship team.

- *Tech Director:* With audio, video, lighting, and setup logistics both in detail and vision, a leader who takes the vision to the screen or speaker is vital.

- *Service Producer:* During the worship service, the details and flow need to be managed by a tactful leader. (The larger the setting, the more this is needed.)

- *Programming Director:* Project manager of the content and details for execution keeps the relationships lubricated with follow-through and planning. It shows love and support to have a well-oiled system for your team.

- *Pastor:* This leader keeps the theology, the definition of the "win" for a weekend, and organizational mission alignment in view—think an Executive Producer who also leads the shepherding issues of the team. This role gives both spiritual and organizational direction.

We will walk through how all of these hats work together to encourage worship leaders and their pastors to cast people in the right roles and to delegate with success. Knowing these roles makes us "administer the gifts with grace," factoring in people's shape and how that applies to leading worship.

A Case for Developing People

If we want to have the right to lead, we need to see changed lives as what qualifies us, not popularity, talent, or profit.

CHAPTER 1

A Case for Developing People

Have you been in a church where you lead less than 100 people in the worship service? I've been there, too. Even though I've had the chance to lead hundreds and thousands, the dozens have often been my staple, as well.

As a worship leader, I have led worship in small settings and large settings. I've helped launch two church plants, lead multiple services, and I've served as the main worship pastor for a few mega-churches. In all those years, I have had quite a few opportunities to make mistakes. Since learning often comes more from the foibles than the successes, I hope that by sharing some of these stories, you won't have to learn the hard way like I did!

When I made the transition to ministry, I basically went from delivering pizzas to working in a mega-church on a staff of six people with more than three hundred volunteers. It did not happen overnight, but it sure feels like it.

It has taken much hard work and personal investment. Along the way, I completed theological training, continued my musical studies beyond music school in private lessons, and served in several churches over the last twenty years. Growing into roles from the church platform to the management boardroom allowed me to learn from some very savvy and gifted leaders. Seeing worship leaders from both personally being one and leading them makes this conversation an important one for me. My hope is that my story and experience will make a difference. So here is a story about why learning the many hats are important.

I was in my twenties and a full-fledged worship leader for the first time for a church plant in a beach town. In fact, it was my honeymoon year. Just months before I had been dating my girlfriend, singing in my church choir, and not planning on any big changes to happen in my life very soon. I did not know what the term "church plant" or "worship leader" meant when a friend and mentor of mine suggested I talk with this young pastor named Tom who was looking for a worship leader to help in his new church plant in San Clemente, California. His enthusiasm and warmth sold me on joining his team, with a stipend just below what an apartment rent would cost. Of course, my then-girlfriend of three years had to go with me and wedding plans commenced. It was not easy to convince my in-laws that this arrangement was solvent. But we loaded up a van and moved to the beach. Yes, that year on the beach was indeed a honeymoon year.

We helped set up the chairs along with the music gear each Sunday morning in this new church. My wife and I would get the church sound system, which was housed in a huge old 1970s station wagon. That might sound strange to have your church PA system in an old car, but we had to rent the local community center for worship and storage is expensive in a beach town. A kind church member allowed us use of the garage and car.

On our first Easter Sunday with the church, we got up late. Panic! As usual, we unloaded the gear out of the tailgate of the wagon and moved it into the community center. But, something was missing in our tardy-induced frenzy. The mixing console seemed to have disappeared out of the car. It was one of those moments that as it is happening in slow motion, you suppose it will be repeated in therapy sessions for Post Traumatic Stress Disorder.

That scary vision was demolished in an instant when I saw one of the most beautiful sites that a young worship leader could have ever set his eyes on. Walking toward the venue was my young wife holding a 12-channel Peavy mixing board in her arms. Her dress moved angelically when she carried the supposedly missing mixer into church that morning. Remember, those old-school mixers were not compact! And she was wearing heels!

This proved to me right then that any worship leader worth his or her salt does not do this alone. We have to have a team. Someone has to have our back. We have to employ people who are willing to be there with us. Getting better at organizing and loving your team by putting leaders and partners in place makes for the best-case scenario for you and your church. You can't do this alone.

Developing people is a must, and this book is designed to give you some tools and ideas that will help you grow your teams. We live in an age where things change. So, we have to navigate more than just what happens during a worship set. There's a lot more than Sunday to worry about. Right?

Not too many of us who lead worship do it solo. If we do, that usually is not by choice. Having a team is what makes leading a shared worship experience even more rich. Also, if you are leading worship on the platform, there is no way you can run the sound, advance slides, and play several instruments at the same time. Trust me, if you are like me, you have already tried this and found that it does not work. At least, it is not sustainable, no matter how many apps help you do these tasks.

In ministry the best solution is always a *person*, not a *technology*. Even with technology, you will need a person to run it, right? God uses people who then use tools.

Let me share with you some biblical and practical teaching on why building into people and delegating is important. I believe this is more than just a preference, since it is clearly taught in the Bible.

It builds the next generation.

2 Timothy 2:2 (NIV)

You have heard me teach things that have been confirmed by many reliable witnesses. Now teach these truths to other trustworthy people who will be able to pass them on to others.

Two points are made in the passage that I want to unveil.

1. We are *CALLED* to pass the torch. Our job is to prepare for that time when we will no longer be around. This means we are to empower others. We are not called to simply build our own position for ourselves, but for the greater good, so if from the start we develop people, our church is served.

2. It is *STRATEGIC* to build into others who will also build into others. Think about it. I am not that great at math, but exponential growth can happen in the small development of one person who then develops another. If we keep developing people and those people do the same, in a short time, the compound interest will mean our church has a solid base to expand and deal with the challenges of the future.

A lot of the frustration from younger people is that they have to cause a revolution in order to express their gifts. This is too often true because many of us who are in the gate-keeping seats keep these positions for ourselves. But the way to stay relevant is to build into others who will do the same.

Let's stop the cycle of revolt and build an attitude of celebrating and empowering others who will take what we have done further. That sounds a lot better than starting from scratch each generation, right?

It makes us credible as leaders.

2 Corinthians 3:1–3 (NIV)

Are we beginning to praise ourselves

again? Are we like others, who need to bring you letters of recommendation, or who ask you to write such letters on their behalf? Surely not! The only letter of recommendation we need is you yourselves. Your lives are a letter written in our hearts; everyone can read it and recognize our good work among you. Clearly, you are a letter from Christ showing the result of our ministry among you. This "letter" is written not with pen and ink, but with the Spirit of the living God. It is carved not on tablets of stone, but on human hearts.

Our resume is the people we build. No matter how great our last worship service was, people are ultimately what's most important. In five years, one single service will not matter, will it? What will?

People will follow you if you shepherd them and feed them. This might mean that instead of just scheduling a slot, we begin to see our teammates as people who need our guidance—especially in regards to leading worship and putting on a weekend experience.

When you make that mistake that you surely will make, it is important to have the relational investment to ensure grace rules. If your people love you for the spiritual change in your life, they are less likely to jockey for position or be unfair to you as their leader. In that way, you build a culture that enables people to follow your example. And, they will follow you—whether it is in your immaturity or your transformative leadership.

If we want to have the right to lead, we need to see changed lives as what qualifies us, not popularity, talent, or profit. How many lives have been changed is more important than the fickle praise of man. We all want praise, sure, but we need to develop people if our goal is changing lives.

You should plan on growth; building people is how you do that.

No matter the size, you need to organize people. Starting that process while small will allow you to do it better and faster as you grow, or as you face deeper challenges. Are you ready for change or planning on retiring already?

We should all plan on replacing ourselves eventually. I once heard this point made years ago: Every pastor is an interim pastor. If you get hit by a bus this week—*God forbid*—your church will still have a worship service the following weekend. That is a fact. Have you planned for that?

If Moses had not received coaching by his father-in-law Jethro, he could not have managed the thousands of Israelites walking through the wilderness and dealt with their relational and civil issues. Like Moses, we likely have more than we can handle on our plate. We need leaders of leaders to expand. All growing churches think this way. The better we get at organizing people so that more are cared for and led well, the more our churches become healthy and grow.

Also, it's interesting to note that David organized worship leaders in a military fashion. Just because you are a "creative," it does not mean you can forgo thinking about organization. If you do, you will end up being the roadblock and bottleneck for God growing your ministry and possibly even your church.

Developing people, whether or not it is in your wiring or experience, is what spiritual lead-

ership is about. And worship leadership is spiritual leadership. With the *Six Hats*, I hope to help you be better equipped to employ and develop the uniquely called and gifted people under your care.

The Pyramid of Execution

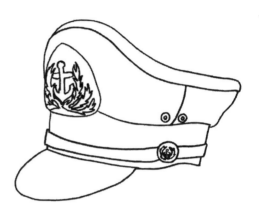

Instead of trying to cover or divert an issue, when you find its foundational identifier, lead from a place of strength and health. Do this and you'll solve the problem many times over in the future, and with second- and third-generation leaders.

CHAPTER 2

The Pyramid of Execution

What is *invisible* is as important as the *visible* in building a healthy, growing, and reproducing worship experience. There are tasks and skills that are easily visible, and those that take more time to actually see. If we want to build a healthy and mature worship and arts ministry, we must be able to be sure the below-the-line ministry people are thought of as much as the above-the-line roles. In this pyramid of execution, I use the metaphor of a pyramid-shaped iceberg to express the value of all that goes on before the visible execution of platform leadership occurs.

The Invisible

The below-the-line roles often get overlooked by both pastors and their worship leaders—until a microphone squeals or a slide is not executed properly. Then the heat is on. In fact, the major cause of anxiety by a teaching pastor in the pulpit occurs when there is not confidence that his or her sermon slides are on cue.

For the up-front worship leader, the same is true. Try teaching a new song when the slides mistakenly advance to the announcements. In this

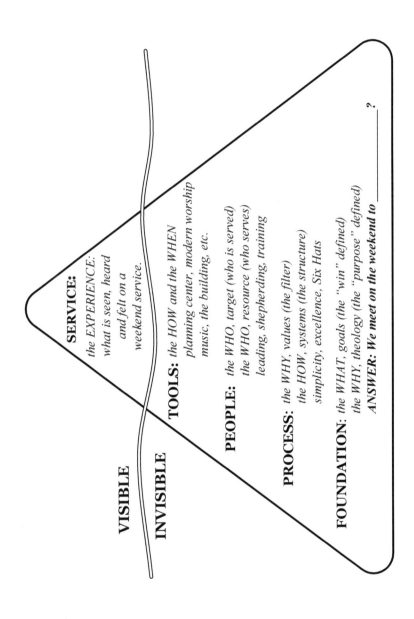

VISIBLE

INVISIBLE

SERVICE: *the EXPERIENCE: what is seen, heard and felt on a weekend service.*

TOOLS: *the HOW and the WHEN planning center, modern worship music, the building, etc.*

PEOPLE: *the WHO, target (who is served)*
the WHO, resource (who serves)
leading, shepherding, training

PROCESS: *the WHY, values (the filter)*
the HOW, systems (the structure)
simplicity, excellence, Six Hats

FOUNDATION: *the WHAT, goals (the "win" defined)*
the WHY, theology (the "purpose" defined)
ANSWER: We meet on the weekend to _____ ?

34

way, the invisible foundation becomes an issue. The house of cards falls because of shifting ground.

The Foundation

The "win" must be defined. I humbly admit that I have seen deer-in-headlight responses from leaders when I have openly asked this question: "What is our goal for the worship service this weekend?" There is nothing that shakes a foundation more than unclear metrics or ones not based on sound theology. We reproduce this uncertainty when we expand our services to another hour, campus, or even to our youth group.

In one season of my career, one of my pastors declared that the metric of attendance and giving were correlated to the success of a weekend worship service. If a pastor preaches with this in mind and the offering plate is not full, he is saying he and his worship leader are failing. The defeated attitude and look on this leader's face as his church remained stagnant resulted from this kind of thinking.

But this was shaky ground because it basically said the purpose of worship was to increase attendance and fill the offering plate. I am pretty sure that is not the purpose, nor the primary goal of our weekend worship. So what is the "win" for a worship service?

I cannot answer that for you, but I can say that when a pastor, the worship leader, and the core of a church can fill in the blank of the following question, a solid foundation is built for executing a service: "We meet each weekend to _____."

Can you and your leaders answer this question with confidence?

The Process

The next level of the invisible factors is your process. The values and systems built to express those values happen here. For instance, do you know why you choose a fast tempo at this point in the service versus something else? Perhaps if you have defined a process that says "our value is to move people in the beginning of our services because humans need movement," then you have set up a decision grid all involved can understand. Your process is to move people as they enter and you all know why.

You value "excellence" so this means you audition people and are honest with them when they are unprepared. A value of simplicity may dictate that your church platform has few lighting changes. If you value people being wowed, then you will evaluate that and make decisions based on how much wow-factor is included in your services.

Values are foundational elements. Unseen is the process of discussing and setting the values in place. Although not visible, value clarification is powerful and necessary to execute something that looks like your vision. This is even more true if you want to duplicate your vision with other people.

The People

Obviously, we in ministry are about people. But it is often easy to get confused when we don't define the separation between who is servicing, and who is being served. There is both a target (the one being served) and a resource (the one serving).

In a team, entitlement creeps in swiftly. "Why am I not scheduled on the audio board as often as he is?" Maybe you have a musician who does not prefer to play with tap delay on his guitar on one of the many U2-influenced worship songs that are popular today. These team members have to be reminded, along with ourselves, that we serve for others first. Our preferences are secondary to the people we are spiritually called to lead in worship.

Once our targeted people are served, then we talk about how our preferences can be integrated. We do not want to forget these; we just want to put them into their proper place. Bottom line: if you want to lead others, you come second—or last!

Here is one last thing about preferences. In order to see your values lived out, you have to teach people these values. When are you training your teams? Your team requires a proper view of each individual's role. Remember, developing people is important. Period.

The Tools

Once our foundation, our process, and our people are organized and clarified, we then make better decisions about the tools we employ. What do I mean by tools? These are the facility and the media we employ. It can also be the style of music we choose, such as modern worship or acoustic instruments.

Even though some tools are "visible," the ones that are not are what we tend to neglect. Planning Center, an excellent and popular tool for planning and scheduling all aspects of worship, may never be known by your congregation members. However, thousands upon thousands in our nation use this tool. The clock at the back of the room serves as a tool to keep time, and honors a value of people's flow and their attention.

If you use a tool like Multitracks.com or Loop Community where your band can rehearse or lead worship with recorded tracks, those resources may not be visible to most people. However, it may greatly improve what you do.

The use of IEM (in-ear-monitors) are meant to be unseen as much as possible. The result of less volume on the platform makes the mix clearer and allows the musicians and worship leader to be in sync. This allows a click track to be heard only by the musical platform leaders. Without it, many teams flounder or sound a bit less focused with our modern worship sound.

The point is this: You need to decide on the most effective tools based on who you are. This comes from having clear values and knowing your goals, and it greatly impacts the visible aspects of worship. Again, to reproduce and scale a ministry, these need to be better defined for your church.

The Visible

When your service is humming, or not, this is what we all evaluate. It is what most people see and hear. So this is usually how we troubleshoot and respond to worship issues and problems. We attack the visible.

I would propose that all the items I listed below the visible line in the pyramid chart are where we find our recurring issues. For instance, when members complain about it being "too loud" we can use the pyramid to find the actual culprit. Is it a tool? Is it people being cast in the wrong roles? Is it that we have not communicated our values clearly enough? Do our congregants and leaders know why we gather each weekend? Does the style of how we mix not match the style we desire?

If there's an issue with the sound, it may seem expedient to set a decibel number, when in reality it's the style of music (a tool) that is not right for the people (the target). Instead of trying to cover or divert an issue, when you find its foundational identifier, lead from a place of strength and health. Do this and you'll solve the problem many times over in the future, and with second- and third-generation leaders. You put heat where it belongs and forge a structure that can lead you to higher levels of execution that you might have once thought impossible or unlikely.

The visible is the product. But, the assembly line is how this product comes to be. Your people, as you train them to execute from purpose, values, and tools, will do better for you. The opposite is simply offering iterative feedback that may be true in its aim, but flawed in its results. Tackle the invisible and you are likely to improve the visible.

The Six Hats Explained

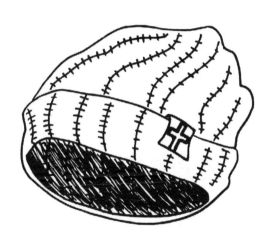

Why choose hats as a metaphor?

You can wear a hat, share a hat, or

give a hat away.

CHAPTER 3

The Six Hats Explained

Why choose hats as a metaphor? *You can wear a hat, share a hat, or give a hat away.*

The idea I have is that these are the same roles I have seen in a church of over 3,000 people, and in a church of under 100 people. If you are planting a church, you need projection and a way to be sure your room is set up. If you have thousands, all of these roles simply become more specialized, professional, and taxing. But the smallest church worship service requires a similar activity each week. You may not have a paid FOH (Front of House audio engineer), but someone still has to take care of the sound system.

Learning to identify these needs and having the willingness to flex with change will allow you to move people in and out of these roles as the needs of your church change. And, you might change, too.

Here are the hats! And as I am explaining each of these roles, my hope is that you can see that one individual is unlikely to have all the skills of the Six Hats under their belt. This is important to note!

Worship Leader

The worship leader's role is the upfront face, an intuitively gifted man or woman who can engage a congregation. There is no doubt that if you cannot get people to follow you from the front, you should probably not be on the platform. That being said, there are three skills this person must have on top of that.

> *Communicator*: A worship leader needs to be a communicator. People understand the content and context as it is delivered with this hat. It makes sense how this person says and sings what they do in front of people. A song leader may be able to get people to sing, but are people clearly being communicated the message of the songs and the purpose for why they are singing?

> *Vocalist*: The first skill in leading singing is that of being a vocalist. People should be able to follow and sing along, and they can clearly understand the words. A lot of people can sing well. However, if a lead singer is too stylized, that may inhibit people from easily

singing along. There is a delicate balance required. Hearing and following a strong singer is what is needed for participation from the church in worship. A simpler singer may be at an advantage. Singing too flat means people may not want to follow or simply cannot hear the pitch.

Direct Flow: The final skill needed is one who can direct flow. When things are electric, this person knows how to adjust the service to move. He or she can read the room and acknowledge on the spot what the congregation is experiencing together. If a song does not connect, it is obvious to the leader. If it isn't, then you may have miscast this hat or role.

Music Director

What does the music director do? The details of music are important, as well as the direction of rehearsal, preparation of charts, and direction of the "sound" of the worship team.

Musical leadership means that there are three areas managed by the one who wears the hat of music director. Each of these has to be in place; if one area is missing, then you can find where some systemic and recurring issues lie. The following three skills are needed for this role to function in a healthy manner.

Arrangement: The musical road map is designed. This is what a musical arrangement does. The tempo, keys, and what each player or singer does is all planned and directed. The tools to coach in music and score music, as well as the collection or creation of tools, all need to be led. Whether you are talking about employing loops or using stock arrangements, there will always be corrections or adjustments needed in the musical road map.

Rehearsal: Running a rehearsal well, or conducting an effective rehearsal, is the hallmark of a good music director. The musical road map and arrangement is applied and prepared together efficiently. Are your rehearsal nights creeping long? Do people come unprepared?

Execution: The music has to be executed well and that is often a personnel issue. Who is on the team? The personnel needs are supervised by the music director so that the right people are in the right places to deliver the musical road map effectively. Which bass player can handle the funky groove in next week's set? That is a musical direction issue.

Tech Director

The tech director hat is audio, video, lighting, and setup logistics, both in detail and vision. Yes, we all get the detail part, but do we see this role as a visionary role? Do we value the need for spiritual leadership? If we do neither, we are not fully casting the work that a tech director needs to do.

Vision means the tech director can foresee the coming needs a church may have when it is time to open a new church campus, or when it is time to upgrade the video system. All the unseen, foundational issues of the Pyramid of Execution are the world that a tech director thrives within.

There are three areas that this role or hat operates within, as far as the weekend services are concerned. Some happen in real-time in service, while others take place completely outside of the weekend.

Setup/Planning: Budgets, scheduling personnel, and training team members need to be owned by the tech director. How are the lines checked for audio before rehearsals? Who is running the screen projection role? How much will it cost to replace a broken amplifier? Are Christmas services staffed? All of these details are closely monitored by the tech director.

Maintenance: Fixing cables, sending gear for repairs, and cleaning equipment all are part of the tech director's realm. A single cable may ruin a weekend. A battery left uncharged chaotically interrupts. Keeping these things humming, no matter how small your church is, matters greatly.

Front of House: Service support and running sound at services is surely a role this individual plays. To train others to do so means he or she has this skill on hand. Otherwise, the spoken word and the musical expression of worship can be hampered. A powerful sermon can be muted by lack of skill. An electric musical time of worship likewise is synergistically accomplished between the tech director and the other five hats.

Service Producer

During the service, the details and flow are managed by the service producer. The larger the setting, the more it seems this is needed, but any size congregation will benefit by having the hat worn that keeps details and flow in line.

What happens if the doors are not closed by the ushers? Are you ready to cue the guest worship leader that he needs to be on the platform? There are so many details in the moment that both need to be managed and followed up. The more this is done, the more chance for improvement.

Also, if you are on the platform, how do you both see and react to all that is going on in the room in real time? You don't because you can't. This is why the service producer is crucial. Communicating and leading hundreds of people requires focus. If that focus is broken with interruption, then both the teacher and the worship leader are less effective.

Liaison: The service producer serves as a liaison before the service for logistics between the worship team and pastor, and Sunday ushers and other support teams. Often, this is all on a sheet from a tool like Planning

Center. The service producer is sure to note that each team member has the information and all are working together. If the worship leader needs to come up early, the service producer retrieves him or her!

Traffic Director: Who will call the cues during service? The more complicated this is, the more the need for this role or hat to be employed. What comes next? How is the timing of the service progressing? Will the service end on time? These are answered and kept by the service producer.

Documenter: Who will document issues from service for improvement or further discussion? Having a way to do this allows those on the platform to do their jobs without the anxiety of wondering who will remember the details that were missed. How long was each of the items in the service? Which of the four services had the volume issue?

Programming Director

The programming director is the administrative project manager of the content and details for execution. He or she keeps the details, scheduling, and project in check. While the service producer is on task during the service, this person has to wear his or her hat completely out of site during the midweek preparations and planning. The three areas of domain for this hat include all that is *organizational*, which can also be categorized as administrative tasks.

Scheduler: The programming director is the master scheduler of personnel, and keeper of project and production timelines. Is the set-list chosen and given to the music director? Is the sermon title ready for the slide for the tech director?

Keeper: The programming director is the keeper of music, resources, and copyrights. Are we legally cleared to use the content we have? Have we gained permission for a video sync to use that specific song on our opener video? Where do we find that song we did last Easter? What is our budget again?

Gatherer: This hat is the gatherer of sermon, songs, service plans, and content for worship. How do we get that fabric for the platform design we want? We need a song about the theme of grace for this service; can you find it for us?

Pastor

The pastor is the shepherd and the executive producer of the weekend worship service. He or she is charged to care for the theology, the definition of the "win" for a weekend, and organizational and missional alignment. This hat also acts as the shepherd of the whole team, and includes both spiritual direction as well as organizational direction.

What happens in my experience is that shepherding is often not pursued to the fullest because the other five hats are poorly worn, or by the time they are, this last one is an afterthought. My hope and goal is to see that the creative and technical servants are spiritually led and organizationally included. This takes three areas being in focus and sustained.

Shepherd: The pastoral role or hat is about growing the ministry deeper. Prayer and the overall spiritual temperature need to be maintained. I have been on and led teams where coarse talk and immature behavior ruled the green room between services. Members would disregard the worship pastor's words. Even worse, entitlement soured the climate with complaints. All of this has to be managed from a pastoral perspective. This takes time and relationships. If the hats are not shared or given away, this one will likely be haphazardly executed.

Visionary: The shepherd of the team must be a visionary leader who can answer the why, not just execute the how. Keeping the team in line with the church's goals and priorities is critical. To see the church's needs grow requires one who can see and track along with the primary leadership's vision and communicate it to those who serve on the weekend.

It does not work to have a team that is predominately subversive. Of course, people are in process and need grace. But are you shepherding them to maturity?

Servant: The pastor is a servant and a supporter. Resourcing the practical needs is also important. And buffering the team from politics and other issues must be factored into the equation of leadership. This hat means that instead of deflecting political heat on your team members, you are able to absorb it or deal maturely with it. Our worship and technical teams can become wounded from friendly fire. Do you have a strategy to keep that from happening? Is someone watching to see that any badly behaving members are thwarted?

Delegating Hats

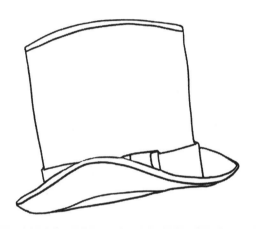

Exposing your holes and filling them with others is how delegating works. You should be a hero by empowering others instead of doing it all, even if you can do it all.

CHAPTER 4

Delegating Hats

The Hats You Wear and the Hats You Give Away

Ultimately, it is clear that in any sized ministry, a single person cannot wear all the hats. Even if one tries, they cannot be worn all at the same time. In order to share, or give away hats or roles, we need to filter that decision.

How do I decide what hats to wear or not wear?

- Be willing to wear more than one hat. No matter the size of your church, you will have to wear more than one hat at the same time. This is normal.

- It is best to be in your strengths. What can I do best? The main hat you have to wear has to be your A-game hat.

- It is necessary at times to fill in for a need. What must be covered that I cannot be without right now? You will sometimes have to wear a hat that is not fun for you, nor will it bring out your A-game. If you are smart, it will not be worn permanently.

- Accept that you will have seasons where holes are not filled completely. And allowing a hole sometimes creates the opportunity to fill it. Plugging everything sometimes keeps people hiding who might otherwise help you.

Exposing your holes opens up the need.

One time I almost lost my job as a new worship leader. We had one drummer who demanded to remain our sole drummer. But the philosophy I presented opposed this, of course. Unhappy with my decision to use other drummers as well, this drummer took our best singer—his wife—and walked away from our church. Yet in six weeks we had three drummers, each one as gifted as the one who walked away.

Had I kept the drummer and not had a hole, those three others would never have come forward. Losing people sometimes opens up a need, and a need is what people respond to. Do you let your church know your holes, or do you hide them?

We all have holes—both in our churches and in our personal skill-sets. In talking about leadership roles, we are frequently guilty of hiding them. Why? If we are the worship leader, it may mean losing our job if we expose our weak points. In unhealthy church leadership settings, pastors and leaders hide any weaknesses. But this is eventually fatal.

The best (and healthiest) strategy is to hold on to the hats you are best at, and communicate effectively the need for others to wear or share the hats you are not so good at. Exposing your holes and filling them with others is how delegating works. You should be a hero by empowering others instead of doing it all, even if you can do it all.

How to Delegate Hats

Start small. If you have a Music Director role to fill, let the person try directing one rehearsal a month. Don't give full responsibility until the person is ready and has proven themselves capable. Observing over time will tell you and those around you the truth about the readiness of a leader.

Invest in and value skill and character. Time must be spent teaching and training. If you have a person who has the skill you're looking for, be sure you know how to spot the skill in the first place. Get advice on assessing if a person has the skill. If you are not an organizer, find a leader in your church to help you discover the markers of what makes a person organized and able to take on responsibility.

Get creative! If you want to find your next vocal music director, put on a music workshop for your church. Training settings can become a magnet and fishing pool for leaders because leaders are attracted to growth and personal development.

Lead Relationally

Take time to be in relationship with other team members and ask these questions only in this order. And remember, one step at a time is how we follow Jesus. Over time, being on the right path with the right people with you will get you where you truly want to go—following Jesus. Anyone and everyone should be helping others take steps. If we are not, we are likely not taking any ourselves.

- Who are you? (What's your story?)

- Where are you spiritually? (Where is your path taking you?)

- How can I help you take your next step? (Here is my story and path; can we follow Jesus together?)

Getting to know someone's story takes purpose. You have to commit to listening and earning the right to hear the unique story of another. This also takes time. But it can be transformative, not only for the one sharing, but for you as that individual's leader. Then, when you have truly listened empathetically, you have the ability to find the spiritual temperature. After that has been on the table, it is in relationship that you offer what might be that individual's next step. It may simply be helping him or her meet someone who can take them further than you can as a leader. But be in relationship so you can speak into the heart and life of your team. If a person does not want a relationship with other team members, that's a red flag.

Steps mean you are willing to walk with those you lead, just as Jesus did. The investment in people is the only way a system or program in ministry has a chance of existing. People are both the product and the means by which ministry is accomplished.

Plan for Feast and Famine

You may leave sooner or later. If you love your family, you should actually prepare for it. For instance, parents should have life insurance policies for their families to care for the worst-case scenarios. It's the same with our churches. Like I mentioned earlier, if you or I get hit by a bus, there will be still be worship in our churches the following weekend without us.

There are fat times and lean times. Joseph in the Bible interpreted Pharaoh's dream, forecasting seven years of plenty and seven years of famine. Storehouses were built and the preparations saved not only Egypt, but people from all over came and bought food.

Every ministry has its cycles. Sometimes setbacks happen, and you will occasionally have to start over. It's not pessimistic or lacking in faith to prepare for the worst, while you expect the best. It is simply being a leader who, like Joseph, plans for these cycles.

When things are fat and your team is cooking along, the tendency is to rest in that and stop recruiting other leaders. But this is the best time to do more training and experimenting that will pay off when the lean season rears its head.

Simply, we need to answer the question: "Who will replace me when I'm gone?" You may not leave, but if you are growing as a church, this question, if answered, will put into place a worship leadership team in a new church plant, a youth group team, a children's ministry worship team, or a new multi-site launch.

Remember, hats are worn, shared, or given away. Use this process and you will likely have more in the lean times. Even better, when your church takes off, the bench—those who you've been mentoring along the way—will be able to offer every type of leadership to every ministry need. Like Joseph, you will be rewarded for thinking this way.

Final Thoughts

If this book has been of help to you, please share it! I invite you to read my blog RKblog.com "Create. Believe. Lead." to dialog with me and other creative leaders just like us. If creatives make you nervous, then you *especially* need to read my blog!

The third thing is an invitation to subscribe to my monthly newsletter. (Simply, go to my site RK blog.com to do that.) For those who have purchased this book, I am offering my email list, additional custom content, and previews of upcoming publications.

The last thing I wish to leave you with is this: Please dialog courageously, creatively, and with passion. I know many are not in "safe" or "healthy" settings as worship or creative leaders. Even if you are on a thriving team, you will have many growth issues to solve. The purpose of this book is to give you permission to lead your leaders and your church by providing a language that facilitates building a healthy culture.

I have not answered all of your issues. I am not that smart. But I have given you what I hope is a tool to solve them on your own with your own tribe.

In order to tackle the tension of leading worship in the local church, an effective language surely will help you navigate your current and future issues. Now that you are enabled with a language to describe worship leadership, you may find relief of some basic frustrations and hopefully freedom to tackle larger issues. Like me, your hats will change over time—depending on ministry needs or even personal stages in life. Yes, wear the hats. But, remember to share some and give some away, too.

Bio

Rich Kirkpatrick, Author

With over 20 years as a professional musician and creative leader, Rich worked as an associate pastor, ministry division manager, church planter, communications director, and worship leader at various churches–from small churches to mega-sized. As a writer, speaker and blogger, his bent is to influence fellow creatives and leaders to help them think strategically with conversations that clarify values, theology, and the practical.

Coaching is something Rich enjoys. Whether it's leading worship ministry, creative volunteers, or implementing social media in a ministry setting, Rich brings his unique experience and knack for conversation to the table. You can find this in his blogging, podcasting, speaking, or hanging out with him at his favorite local coffee shop.

Rich is also a worship leader and singer-songwriter. He recently released a song with the project

Missional Music Volume One, and in March of 2012 released a five-song EP titled "Drink The Divine" of all original material. Rich's songs are published with Epic Stache Music (ASCAP).

A native of San Jose, California, Rich currently resides in beautiful Temecula, California, with his wife Tammy who is Head of School at a Southern California charter school. They have two children.

- Email Rich at rich@rkblog.com

- Blog (RKblog.com)

- Twitter at @rkweblog

- Facebook.com/RichKirkpatrick

Made in the USA
Middletown, DE
27 April 2016